Falkirk's Trams
and
Early Buses

A.W. Brotchie

Public transport before the tramway or internal combustion engine was provided in the Falkirk area by a number of coach-masters who operated these small brakes. Normally open to the elements, in winter and during wet weather a rudimentary hood was fitted. Owners included McLaren Brothers and John Reid of Stenhousemuir, plus J Borthwick and W Wyse of the Royal Hotel and many others. So many operators brought out their conveyances, particularly on market days, that in 1901 the burgh police calculated that 73 horse-drawn passenger vehicles were in operation locally, varying in size from accommodating seven passengers, to large 36 seat chars-a-banc. Here one of these typical small open wagonettes is seen crossing the old wooden bascule bridge over the Forth and Clyde Canal at Bainsford. The two section opening structure had remained basically unchanged since the opening of the Canal in 1773. It was of such limited carrying capacity as to require additional support – provided by a barge floated below – whenever a load greater than 3 tons weight was to be transported across.

Text © A.W. Brotchie, 2011.
First published in the United Kingdom, 2011,
by Stenlake Publishing Ltd.
54-58 Mill Square,
Catrine,
KA5 6RD

Telephone: 01290 551122
www.stenlake.co.uk

ISBN 9781840335460

The horse wagonette performed a useful service, but was hardly adequate transport for the growing burgh entering the twentieth century. This horse bus standing outside the old County Buildings at the west end of Newmarket Street is probably for Bonnybridge or Larbert.

An open wagonette petrol-engined omnibus of the type used to initiate services by the Falkirk & District Motor Car Co Ltd in May 1898. The 4½ horse power Daimlers were imported from Germany and then had an eight seat body, with a further two seats beside the driver, constructed in Hamilton (Lanarkshire) by J and C Stirling. It then commanded a price of £355 as a 'private omnibus', a not inconsiderable amount, equivalent in the early twenty-first century to some £150,000 (if the comparison is based upon average earnings). The thirteen vehicles owned when the service ceased were auctioned off and found further use with other operators. One is still in existence (later registered as MS172 and exhibited in Edinburgh's one-time transport museum at Shrubhill) which achieved the distinction of being sold by auction at Sotheby's in 1965, and which subsequently participated in the London to Brighton veteran car run.

Introduction

Falkirk never participated in the first generation of (generally) horse-drawn trams, but just ten miles away was to be found the venerable service which had provided transport between the eponymous county town, Stirling, and its neighbouring spa of Bridge of Allan. From 1874 this first generation line served unremarkably, until in the tramway 'mania' which swept the United Kingdom following the successful adoption of electric power as the prime mover, it seemed ripe for modernisation, and several schemes were put forward – the first near the end of the nineteenth century.

Perhaps at this time the entrepreneur of the day cast his eye upon the cluster of hamlets around the industrial centre of the county at Falkirk. Here a population of over 20,000 was swollen to over 50,000 when surrounding settlements were included. Indeed the size of the town was greatly increased when the previously independent villages of Laurieston, Bainsford, Grahamston and Camelon were absorbed into the burgh in 1900. However, even by this date the transport needs of the area had been assessed, and a company was formed by local businessmen to operate motor wagonettes on a regular timetable. This venture – the Falkirk and District Motor Car Company Limited – began its service on 2nd May 1898, one of a number of similar operations which sprang up at that time in Scottish communities. These were among the very first such operations in the world of motor vehicles for hire. Falkirk had motor buses before it had trams; not many places can claim this distinction.

The vehicles used were eight seat Daimler wagonettes supplied by J & C Stirling of Hamilton in Lanarkshire who also built the bodies. The first three ran a route approximately every hour from Newmarket Street in Falkirk to Carron Works and on to Stenhousemuir. When more vehicles were to hand this was extended to the 'circle' – by Larbert and Camelon back to Falkirk. With fares rising to 6d for the round trip, the service was effectively outwith the pocket of the working man (at the turn of the century an agricultural worker's wages would be less than 6d per hour). By the end of 1900, when the company was forced out of business following legal proceedings, thirteen vehicles were owned, and operations extended to serve Polmont, Bonnybridge and Carronshore. For a short period thereafter local transport reverted to the horse bus and wagonette, but plans for an up to date electric tram service were in hand.

In 1901 Parliamentary approval was given for the Falkirk and District Tramways Order Confirmation Act, out of the proposed capital of £250,000 less than half was raised and the local authorities involved found that the agreed wayleave payments never appeared. After three years of inaction, an option for the powers to build was acquired by Messrs Bruce Peebles & Co of Edinburgh who formed the Falkirk Electric Construction Syndicate Ltd which immediately entered into a contract with [surprise, surprise] Bruce Peebles to build the tram line. No further delay was countenanced and ground was broken in January 1905, with power to be provided from the nearby power station recently constructed by the Scottish Central Electric Power Co – another enterprise funded by Bruce Peebles Ltd. With some haste work progressed, with the formal opening on Saturday 21st October 1905.

While the track round the circle from Falkirk via Carron, Stenhousemuir, Larbert, Camelon and back to Falkirk, was complete, a dispute with the owners of the Forth & Clyde Canal – over which the tramway was carried by two opening bridges – prevented the circle to be operated as such for some months. However, this was eventually overcome and with traffic returns increasing, authority was obtained for extensions of the line to Laurieston and Grangemouth. Road widening (and other) disputes delayed the latter, but work on the line to Laurieston was put in hand, with that branch opening on 3rd September 1909. This line was always worked as a separate entity from the circle line, it being considered that the west end of Falkirk's High Street was too narrow for tram operation.

This little system, with its eighteen cars served the needs of the area well, but the shortcuts taken in initial procurement soon came to light, with track and vehicles both requiring more attention than should have been necessary. The First World War changed the nature of the service provided, with the need to function with reduced manpower, but to supply transport needs to the large number of munitions – and other – workers who were concentrated in this industrialised area.

Before the war the tramway company had bought its first charabanc, and when the war ended this side of the business rapidly expanded. The first regular route run was to Grangemouth, from 1st January 1915. After the war, bus services mushroomed, with many ex-services chassis suddenly on the market, and local operators were not slow to take advantage. One Walter Alexander, based at Brown Street in Camelon had actually purchased his first vehicle in 1914, and was also able to expand, using ex-RAF motor chassis.

In 1920 financial control of the local tramway company passed into the hands of the Fife Tramway, Light and Power Company, part of the Balfour-Beatty Group. The FTL&PCo had been incorporated to construct and operate the Dunfermline tramways, with the power supply controlled through the associated Fife Electric Power Co. These four companies had similar aims, and both of the tramway companies had omnibus departments which were rapidly expanding. The Scottish General Omnibus Company had been formed in December 1919 to develop the Falkirk tramway's bus operations. Consequently the bus side of the Dunfermline tramways was now absorbed as a part of the SGOCo. The FTL&PCo saw a good and profitable future for their two tramways and both systems saw the benefits of reconstructed track layouts and (in Falkirk only) new vehicles. Large sums were invested in the new track, much of this work attracting funding from Unemployment Alleviation Grants in this time of unemployment and depression of trade following after the end of the First World War. The Laurieston branch had declining use and suffered badly from bus competition which was easily able to expand to serve the various settlements to the south. It was not reconstructed and the service was abandoned after 20th July 1924 – the first such electric tramway closure in Scotland.

Further changes in July 1929 saw the power generation side of the company (with the two major coal-fired power stations at Bonnybridge and Townhill) sold to the Scottish Central Power Company, leaving the FTL&PCo to deal with road transport only – now a major operation in its own right with 64 trams and over 300 buses, and serving a geographical area through acquired companies stretching through central Scotland and also between Inverness and Aberdeen. However, this also was revised in a major fashion from June 1930 when the bus operations were sold to the Scottish Motor Traction Co who immediately transferred operations to their subsidiary, Walter Alexander Ltd – who had been absorbed by SMT during the previous year. All these changes were triggered by the effects of the four separate Railways (Road Transport) Acts of 1928 which allowed the four major railway companies to operate road passenger services, the corrosive effects of unfettered omnibus competition having severely affected their passenger numbers. The rail companies chose to achieve their ends by purchasing into the existing established industry and in Scotland, their nominee was the SMT Company. In turn this organisation, largely through the personal efforts of its Chairman, (later Sir) William J Thomson, devolved operational matters into several large regional companies. Of these – and again probably as a result of a direct personal relationship – the 'vehicle' chosen for operations throughout most of central Scotland and as far north as Aberdeen was the existing business operated by Walter Alexander and his son.

Through all this upheaval the two tramway companies remained, now as the sole operating elements of the FTL&PCo; and so it continued, but the tramways were seen from a distance as an anachronism responsible for filtering off much profitable traffic from the (monopoly) bus undertaking – in 1934 the circle carried 3,776,319 fare paying passengers, the largest figure achieved in the post-war period. This state of affairs could not be allowed to continue, hence in early 1935 the SMT megalith made an offer to purchase the issued shares and within a short time had acquired over 99% of the stock. Immediately negotiations with the local authorities involved were commenced. When these were completed it was rapidly announced that transport services in the Falkirk area were to be rationalised and improved; the date for closure of the Falkirk tram circle was fixed as 21st July 1936.

This date duly arrived and the last tram – not even ten years old – ran round the familiar circular route. The following day Alexander's blue double deck buses were the only means of public transport round the route. Today, some 75 or so years later, the Alexander's name no longer graces the sides of the modern single deck successors on the circular route; but the circle remains a busy service, indicating that even after this time lapse, the vision of transport requirements as seen in the closing years of the nineteenth century remains valid.

The generous assistance of the Falkirk Council Archives department staff is gratefully acknowledged, as is the help of George Heaney, Guthrie Hutton, Brian Longworth, Mrs B McCutcheon, Ian Scott and Alan Simpson.

A.W. Brotchie, April 2011

The easily accepted circular route linking local settlements passed several bridges, two over the Forth and Clyde Canal, two below the North British Railway at Camelon Station and two over the River Carron. The famous Carron Ironworks had, from the eighteenth century been connected to local collieries by primitive wooden-railed waggonways, but in 1810 an iron-railed waggonway on stone block sleepers was laid from the works to Bainsford Basin on the Forth and Clyde Canal. This remarkable old

scene shows the original (1775) stone bridge over the River Carron just to the south of Carron Works, with, on its upstream side the iron bridge built to carry the waggonway. The last remaining rails of this waggonway, which was of double track from end to end, can be discerned in the left foreground. The short rails would, with little doubt, have been cast in the adjacent ironworks and it will be noted that there appear to be no curved rails, the bend merely having been formed by a succession of straight rails. Horses were used to pull waggons to and from the canal basin, the rail gauge being said to be about four feet. The track became disused soon after 1858 when a branch was built connecting the works to the 'main line' of the Stirlingshire Midland Junction Railway near Camelon, when the waggonways around the works and nearby coal pits were altered to the 'standard' gauge.

The two old bridges were demolished and replaced in 1905 by a new structure built specifically to carry the planned electric tramway. This view looking downstream shows particularly clearly the iron waggonway bridge built in 1810, and which was attached to the side of the older stone construction. According to C F Dendy Marshall in his *History of British Railways down to the year 1830*, the iron girders extended right through the stone arches to the other side. It is a great pity that the historical nature of the old iron bridge was not appreciated in 1905 and its demolition prevented. It could be that the waggonway gauge influenced the promoters of the Falkirk electric tramways, as they specified the same gauge for their new lines detailed in the Parliamentary Bill and its deposited plans of 1901. This was the only tramway constructed to this gauge in Scotland, and its choice is otherwise unexplained. The replacement bridge cost of £3,850 was paid by Falkirk Council, assisted by contributions of £750 from the Tramway Company and £250 from the Carron Company.

Construction of the electric tramway started in early 1905, the first load of rails being delivered in January. Work commenced in Larbert and was executed swiftly – no problem then to accommodate other road traffic. By the end of June this was the scene at the locus then known as Guildybutts, just south of Carron Iron Works which can be seen in the distance. On the left is the raised track-bed which formerly carried the waggonway from the works to Bainsford Basin while beyond the wall the blast furnaces of the iron works can be made out. Beside the old culvert exposed passing below the disused waggonway formation is the board of the main contractor Messrs Bruce, Peebles & Co Ltd of Edinburgh. They were electrical engineers, responsible also for tramways in the Sunderland District, at Llandudno, plus several overseas installations including Singapore and Athens. Their main interest involved the electrical generation and distribution, plus supply of traction motors etc. Other elements of the work were subcontracted, track laying to Messrs A G Whyte of London.

The owners of the Forth & Clyde Canal, by this time (from 1867) the Caledonian Railway, proved difficult in negotiations with the fledgling tramway company. Their old wooden bascule bridges at Bainsford and Camelon were by this date inadequate for the road traffic of the time, but this did not prevent the railway company from driving a hard bargain. Completely new swing bridges were required, and despite the benefit to the canal's owners it was their demand that the entire cost of the new bridges be borne by the tramway promoters. The new bridges were designed to accommodate a load of sixteen tons, considerably more that just the weight of a crossing tramcar. Construction of the two canal bridges was also subcontracted; in this case the steelwork was by the Motherwell Bridge Company, and electrical work by the Bridge Electric Equipment Company of London.

Erection of poles to support the tramway overhead electric wires proceeded in parallel, but after, track construction. This scene was recorded in Larbert Road near the old corn mill building (just visible in the distance and powered by the water of the River Carron which flowed just behind the trees on the north east side of the roadway). It shows how the horse-drawn tower wagon was a necessity to add the finishing touches. The worker on the top platform is standing on the handrail – in a manner which would cause today's health and safety inspector to have a heart attack – to install the 'ball-and-spike' finial which sits on top of the pole to seal the open end. His colleague on terra firma is attaching a rope to one of the cast iron rings which serve to cover and protect the joints of the pole. Supervising all is the resident engineer Douglas Hays in his jaunty straw boater head wear. He still manages to appear dapper after climbing to the top platform in his 'working clothes'.

Meantime construction of the depot building on a two acre green-field site at the appropriately named Carmuirs, between Camelon and Larbert was well under way, with erection of the steel-framed structure progressing. Needless to say the working practices adopted clearly demonstrate how attitudes to safety have changed. Indeed

this could represent an ideal example of how not to do it! The ladder is a potential death trap; it has a missing rung and its method of construction has been taboo for years. The two erectors aloft would be quite at home in the rigging of a sailing ship! Construction of the maintenance pits for the trams is well advanced, with the longitudinal timbers in place to which the rails will be attached. Perhaps the site was convenient from the operational point of view, but it was in the wilds as far as convenience for staff was concerned, with no handy adjacent housing. The open site did have one major long-term advantage when, in years to come, it was able to expand readily to accommodate the needs of the growing company.

TRACK LAYOUT AS CONSTRUCTED

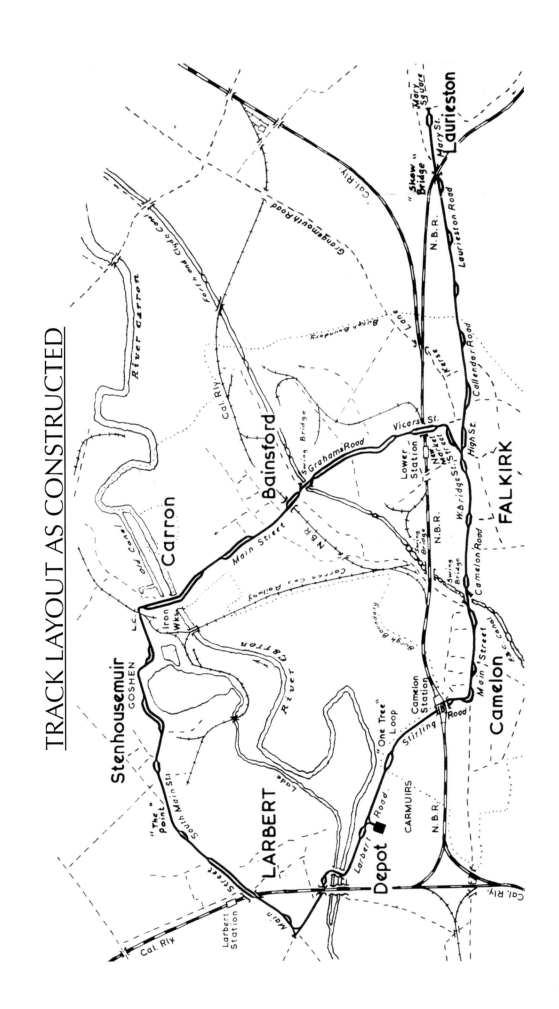

The rural nature of the depot location is apparent in this August 1905 scene probably taken from the top of the tower wagon. This is actually the field adjacent to the depot, where advantage has been taken of the space available to make a trial assembly of the bits and pieces of rail required to form the depot access tracks. An entrance from both directions off the main line formed a triangle which provided a suitable facility for the trams to be turned end-for-end – a procedure necessary (particularly since the route was a circular one) – to equalise wear on the flanges of the wheels of the cars. Behind the track display can be seen the trucks of the cars, again taking advantage of the unrestricted available space.

Another triangular junction was provided at Larbert Cross, seen here in course of construction, looking west. Not really necessary for operational reasons, several alternative explanations have been postulated for its creation. About this time there was talk of a tramway connection between the Falkirk District Tramways here at Larbert, via Plean, Cowie and Bannockburn to meet a reconstructed Stirling tramway – and even to extend as far as Dunblane, also to link Alva, Tillicoultry and Dollar. It would appear to have been a tad premature to construct the junction on the basis of such a potential, which was never realised probably as a result of changed transport provision after the First World War. Another suggestion was that it may have been considered that the radius of the curve on the 'direct' line was too tight for normal operation, but this was soon proved perfectly satisfactory for every day use. Yet another thought was that this stub on the Stirling Road was to act as a terminus for short working cars. No evidence has been found that this ever took place. The Red Lion pub on the right of the picture is probably the only unchanged feature in the scene, the rival Commercial (the former White Hart) on the opposite corner demolished to allow for road widening and re-alignment. In the nineteenth century the other two corners also supported inns, the Eagle and the Wheatsheaf, and if locals were still drouthy, the Railway Tavern was just 100 yards down the street!

Meantime the order for the tram cars had been sub-contracted by the main contractor, Messrs Bruce Peebles, (who nevertheless supplied their own make of traction motor for the cars). They were built in St Denis, France, by the Compagnie Générale de Construction, and in use quickly proved to be very poorly constructed. The French-built cars arrived in Scotland in two batches, the first on the SS *Dunavon* arriving into Grangemouth Docks on 18th July 1905, the second during the first week of August. Car No. 1 is pictured at the manufacturer's works, looking pristine in its cobalt blue paintwork (one source states the dash plates were painted brown, but there is no tonal variation in any of the many remaining photographs to suggest this).

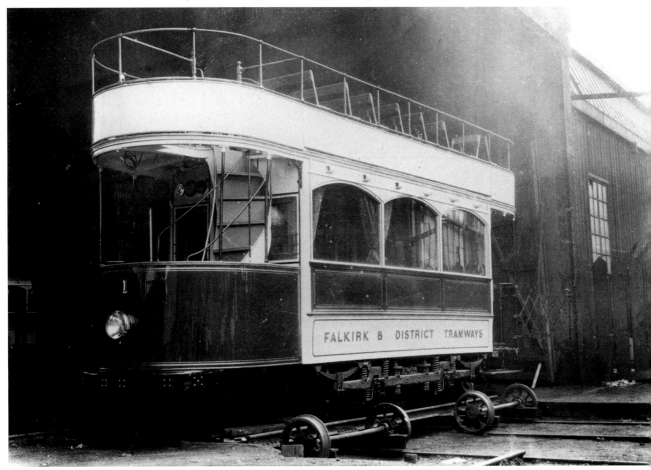

When fabricated, the French cars had a builders' plate fixed in an unusual, but very noticeable, place in the centre of the step on to the platform, but there is no sign of this in any subsequent photograph. The implication is that these plates were removed before the cars went into service, and while the contemporary local press gives full detail of the cars' French ancestry, all references in the technical press of the day unusually omit any reference to their builder. Without exception these journals use illustrations, not of one of the fifteen French cars, but of one of the three British-built cars added to the order and supplied by the Brush Electrical Engineering Company of Loughborough. It may well have been the case that British manufacturers were unable to supply the vehicles to the accelerated demands of the tramway company, but the decision to buy French was one which was to be bitterly regretted in a few short months.

A scene of intense activity in July or August 1905, at the yet incomplete depot at Carmuirs on the Larbert road. While the basic shed is advanced to a stage where the newly arrived cars can be worked on under cover, work on the offices and ancillary accommodation to the right has yet to commence. The cars are in a 'knock-down' state for transportation, with the top deck seats inside the saloon and the top deck panels dismantled. Pairs of wheels are lying, to be assembled with motors into the French-built trucks. Two motors of 30 horse power were fitted to each car.

Although Bruce, Peebles supplied the traction motors, it is believed they were made under licence by Ganz of Budapest in Hungary. Needless to say, little or no acknowledgement of this was made publicly, but this company is one of the few which were involved with the Falkirk tramway which is still in existence.

Bruce, Peebles major interest was in the supply of electrical equipment; they were instrumental in the establishment of many power generating plants and the founding of power supply companies. Their Scottish Central Electric Power Company built a large coal-fired power station at Bonnybridge, just three miles west of Camelon where an electric tramway nearby would have been an ideal and steady customer for power. Unfortunately Falkirk Council, who had just invested in their own generating plant, thought the same and tortuous negotiations held up decision making. The tram company had an agreement to purchase power from the SCEP Co at 1¼d per unit, but it was realised at a late stage that the SCEP Co had no authority to supply within Falkirk's (newly extended) boundary. Falkirk's rate for supply was considered outrageous and the dispute was to be referred by the Burgh to the Court of Session. By the beginning of October no compromise had been achieved, but the trams were ready to run; trial running of the first cars commenced on 23rd September 1905.

Falkirk's tramway came along at exactly the right time for the picture post card publisher, and there are many cards which record this indication of how modern the town had just become. Postcard manufacturers were quick off the mark, and this card showing brand new car 10 in Camelon Main Street bears a message referring to the occasion depicted: *This is our first trial car can you pick me out I am there somewhere hope your all keeping well …* The card was posted to Leith on 30th September 1905, remarkably only just one

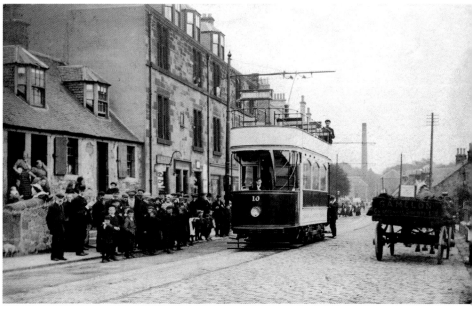

week after the actual event took place. One young lad has managed to get on the platform to be recorded for posterity. All buildings to the left of the scene between the top of Dorrator Road and the canal have disappeared; the street now a busy dual-carriageway. The Rosebank Distillery chimney in the background is the only landmark remaining. On the right, the Camelon Co-operative Society cart delivering coal.

The question of supply of power within the boundaries of Falkirk burgh was resolved, with the power company undertaking to pay an annual charge to the burgh of £30, plus a one-off sum of £100 to cover legal costs. On the appointed day (21st October) two trams with the provost, town council, and other invited guests on board left the burgh buildings then proceeded round the circle. Public service commenced immediately afterwards (although operation over the canal bridges was not immediately permitted). A sizeable number of onlookers has gathered here on Graham's Road, where the width allowed for construction of double track.

The town council's special car passing Carron Works on their official first day trip. The car (No. 2) is actually crossing over the new bridge spanning the River Carron, which, as can be seen, is almost – but not quite – complete. This stretch of road has since been bypassed to provide a new layout and remove the awkward right-angled bend at the north-east corner of the iron works. Most of this world famous works has now been demolished, but use of the site went back to 1760 when Messrs. Roebuck, Garbett and Cadell chose this location for their new ironworks and then named it after the river which

supplied the necessary water for the process. The manufacture of naval cannon – the 'Carronade' – ensured that the name was known (and feared) across the seven seas.

At Carmuirs Depot, probably also photographed on the opening day, 21st October 1905. Only seven of the total complement of cars are 'on shed', and of those identifiable, neither Nos. 2 or 10 (which were the two cars with the official party) are in the picture. In the dark recesses on the right can be seen two of the Brush-built cars, with one on jacks and still to have its truck fitted. The six tracks could accommodate 22 cars, but the company never achieved this total. The newly-recruited staff pose stiffly in their unaccustomed uniforms, the cars are pristine, unadorned by advertisements and unscuffed by any traffic dust or mud. Car No. 3 in the foreground has a paper bill in the centre window announcing it as a 'Workman's Special'. From the very start of operations considerable revenue was earned from operation of such special workers' cars from Carron and other works.

The truck for one of the Brush-built trams was photographed outside the depot prior to being fitted in place. Trucks under the fifteen French cars were similar, but obviously not of equal construction as all were replaced within three years by new trucks purchased from Messrs. Hurst Nelson of Motherwell. At either end are the wooden slatted life guards, designed to prevent any possibility of a pedestrian involved in an accident being injured by the wheels. In normal operation these were lifted above the road surface, but if an obstruction hit the 'gate' below the leading end of the car, the tray dropped to catch it. Between the wheels are the traction motors, one to each axle, and other details may be seen, including the spring system which carried the body of the car on the truck.

For most of their publicity the main contractor, Bruce, Peebles used illustrations of the British supplied equipment, although this accounted for less than 20% of the total. Thus this record photograph was of car No. 18, one of the three supplied by the Brush Electrical Engineering Company of Loughborough. Seen in pristine condition opposite the depot entrance at Carmuirs, the rural nature of the setting is again apparent. These three cars were much more satisfactory in every aspect, and required much less maintenance and repair. The livery was cobalt blue with white panels – the top deck decency board appear on these cars to have been painted in a distinguishing colour, possibly a paler shade of blue. Unfortunately, while looking extremely smart when freshly applied, blue paint (at that time) was notoriously difficult to maintain and quickly became flat and discoloured.

Another one of the three Brush-built cars (No. 17) was used in this photograph to indicate that the sharp corner round Larbert Cross did not present any real hazard to operation of cars using the shortest side of the triangle. The residents of the tenement on the corner – which still exists – would quickly become familiar with the squeal of the trams' wheel flanges on the curves as the cars rounded the sharp curve. Some towns used automatic flange lubrication on sharp curves to minimise noise; this of course also had the more practical benefit of reducing wear and tear on the wheels. It is thought that this view was also recorded on the

first day of official operation. The complete line had been inspected and passed by the representative of the Board of Trade (a necessity before use by the public was sanctioned) on 17th and 18th October 1905.

A line-up of French cars at Carmuirs Depot in the early months of operation. This interesting and possibly unique postcard was sent in December 1905 to a medical practitioner in Govan, the inscription reading, *I am learning electric car driving in addition to my clerical duties here and find it an excellent tonic and recreation. You would not know your former neurotic patient. I'll try and make a lantern slide of this for you …* Whether or not the tram driving experience continued so pleasurable during the forthcoming winter we shall never know. Tram drivers had no protection from the elements, and their exposed position left them subject to all the extremes of weather.

The view north from Camelon Station along the Stirling Road during the first winter of operation. Mud and 'glaur' covers the roadway away from the paved central area where the tramway was required to lay setts between the track and for a width of eighteen inches on either side. This onerous burden was faced by all tramways and was a throwback to the days of legislation relating to horse tramways, when the road surface on either side of the tracks was necessarily paved for use by the 'motive power'. This was the condition of the main highway between Falkirk and the north. The scene is today much 'improved', with Carmuirs Golf Clubhouse to the left and its large car park on the right. The depot at Carmuirs is just out of sight beyond the far bend of the road to the left – again emphasising the rural nature of its location. The tram in the distance is approaching the camera; its trolley is on the right hand wire. While the track here was only a single line, the overhead wire was generally double so that at passing places there was no conflict from cars going in opposite directions.

At the junction of Stirling Road and Glasgow Road the tramway made a right angled turn to the east, with these early nineteenth century artisans' houses of Redbrae Terrace on the west side of the first mentioned road. They were demolished in the early years of the twentieth century, then tangible relics of the time when Camelon was renowned as a centre for nail-making. The cottage industry, where every nail was hand-made, was overtaken by industrial manufacture, but the old industry is remembered in the present day Nailer Road in Camelon. Nothing remains to recall these old dwellings, the site now cleared and landscaped.

Two cars pass on the loop in Camelon Main Street. That this scene was photographed shortly after the opening of the tramways is indicated by neither of the trams having advertisements on the upper deck panels. This additional means of income was soon introduced, and individual cars became 'personalised' and immediately identifiable by the adverts carried. At the foot of Union Road on the right, the only remaining building which can be recognised today is the three storey block on the east side of the junction. In common with much of Camelon, most other buildings were bulldozed in the sixties and seventies, to be replaced by up-to-date but unremarkable dwellings which could be part of any conurbation from Colchester to Cowdenbeath. Camelon Main Street is now dual carriageway, with few of its old familiar features still recognisable.

Roman Buildings at the foot of Mansionhouse Road Camelon were typical of the second generation of workers' houses in the formerly separate settlement; Camelon was not incorporated into the Burgh of Falkirk until the boundary extensions of 1900. The first construction was generally of very basic single-storey nail-makers

cottages, and in many cases these were replaced early in the twentieth century with three storey tenements of the style generally shown here. They were conveniently situated for travel by the new tramway, and the photographer may have waited specifically until one of the trams was passing. The name 'Mansionhouse' derives from this having originally having been the access to Camelon House, while 'Roman Buildings' would commemorate the close proximity of the Roman Antonine Wall. The street is now a cul-de-sac, without access to the main road, while the new sheriff court building is to the right.

Camelon Main Street, with an 'English' car (now decked out with enamelled sheet metal advertisements) approaching. On the nearby overhead pole there is a car stop sign. These 'flags' (and the advertising panels) were made locally by the Falkirk Iron Company who supplied these (or similar) enamelled signs to local authorities and transport undertakings throughout the world. The wording and colours used could be standardised, or varied to suit the customer's individual requirements. Generally the convention was white letters on a red background, but some purchasers had white on a blue background. Virtually nothing of this scene remains today. Even the road layout has been reconstructed as dual carriageway.

At the east end of Camelon Main Street the tramway crossed the Forth and Clyde Canal and new bridges were necessary for the two places where the tramway met and crossed the canal. The Caledonian Railway Company, owners of the canal since 1867, had no real interest in its well-being or prosperity. They were railway operators, and any canal was a competitor for bulk shipments, although the canal lost out as soon as railway connections were provided to the many industries which had sprung up along the sides of the canal. The railway company were therefore in no position to treat the new tramway company equatibly and immediately objected to the way in which the tram company had built the overhead support work adjacent to the canal bridges. The manner in which these had been built obstructed the tow path of the canal and the railway company were able to prohibit use of the new bridges until such time as their demands were agreed to. This 'reflective' study, looking north, indicates the original pole positions, and the railway level crossing type gates which closed across the roadway when the canal bridge was opened.

Movement of the bridge was by an electric winch driving a cable which ran round a pulley under the centre of the moveable bridge span. There was also an arrangement whereby in the event of a power failure the span could be wound open by hand. Using the motor the opening operation was timed to take less than a minute. The facility was available on a twenty-four hour basis, but no traffic was permitted on Sundays. Openings were frequent and on many occasions caused severe disruption to tramway frequencies. No footbridge facilities were provided for pedestrians who had to make a detour to cross at the closest lock gates at Lock 11, fortunately not too far off.

An early and unusual view of the Camelon Canal Bridge; the barrier across the left-hand end of the structure would suggest that work is not yet complete, and certainly the original overhead poles on the east bank of the waterway are still of the early and unsatisfactory design. The supply of electricity to the trams' overhead was arranged so that before the bridge could be opened, all power was shut off for a distance of 100 yards on either side. In addition, a 'catch-point' arrangement was provided so that a set of points opened to derail any errant tram before it ended up in the canal. There is no record of any such event, although there is at least one incident where a tram driver was disciplined for driving into the 'dead' stretch and having his car thrown off the track!

Tram operation may have commenced as advertised on 21st October 1905, but with use of the two canal bridges prohibited, the service was run as two separate elements on either side. Trams were supposed to be co-ordinated to meet so that passengers could transfer readily on foot across the bridges, but this seemed to be more a theoretical solution than a practical one. The benefits of the new circular tramway  were thus not immediately achieved. This situation prevailed for some 21 weeks until, after negotiation, new support poles were built located at the rear of the tow path, to the satisfaction of the railway company. From 12th March 1906 the tramcars were allowed to cross the two bridges and the circular service commenced operation. The poorest service was a car every fifteen minutes in each direction round the circle, but these were augmented by additional cars operating over parts of the route only. The new cantilever overhead support can be seen on the right side, with the tram now allowed to proceed across the bridge.

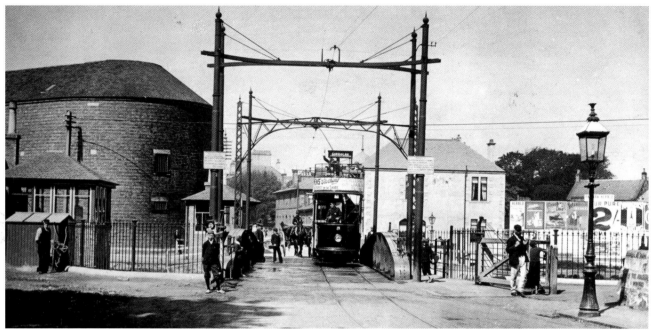

French-built car No. 3 heads east across Camelon Canal Bridge early in 1906. Most of the track was constructed as single line with passing places situated strategically where the cars were timetabled to meet. However, it was a not infrequent occurrence for delays to interfere with the schedule and tram drivers had to make a guess as to whether or not they could make it to the next loop before meeting the coming car. When two cars did meet on single track, it was a written rule that the one which was nearest a loop had to reverse. Too bad for any passenger in a hurry…

Camelon Road, looking east towards Falkirk, again in the early years of tram operation, an area of genteel sandstone villas, with the B-listed Arnotdale House (built 1832) behind the high wall on the north (left) side of the roadway. With the wall reduced in height, this is now the location of the town's war memorial, in the beautiful gardens of Dollar Park (named in remembrance of Robert Dollar who gifted the house and its policies to the burgh). Formerly a museum, the pre-Victorian house was also at one time the home of Robert Barr of the famed soft drinks family. Close by, on the corner of Maggie Wood's Loan on the right side of the scene, was later to be built 'Dakar', home of bus entrepreneur Walter Alexander – complete with stained glass windows which incorporated bluebirds, the instantly recognisable symbol of his company.

The tramway had a loop line in West Bridge Street, just outside the old County Buildings. Although some of the structures on the left side of the street – and out of sight in this view – still exist, almost everything in the photograph has now gone. The only link with the past is the furthest away two storey block on the corner of Wellside Place which still stands. The entire remaining side of West Bridge Street is now occupied by the flat featureless facade of the Central Scotland Police Falkirk headquarters.

At the point where West Bridge Street ran on to the end of the narrow High Street, the tramway made a sharp left turn into Newmarket Street. The later extension of the line to serve Laurieston formed a junction here and ran straight ahead. However, due to the restrictions, no through service operated and the line was used only to get the Laurieston cars to and from the depot. The distinctive Royal Bank building dating from 1879 still surveys the junction, now a busy crossroads since the houses on the right were cleared to allow the 1927 creation of Cockburn Street. The fanciful drinking fountain was erected in 1871 by Bailie John Gentleman, but became a traffic obstruction.

The Gentleman fountain at the extreme west end of the High Street, with its cast iron dome and marble columns all topped by a flightless dove, was removed about 1927 when Cockburn Street was formed. Its unique design should perhaps have ensured its re-erection elsewhere, but unfortunately at that time of civic philistinism, it was merely torn down to be scrapped. Bailie Gentleman paid for it, but it was built by his brother, Patrick. Behind it can be seen tram No. 2 proceeding into Newmarket Street on its anticlockwise circular route. On several occasions, for example during the annual Tryst Fair, to avoid delays incurred by cars having to wait at the passing places, all trams operated in one direction (anti-clockwise) ensuring a very frequent service from Falkirk to the grounds at Stenhousemuir, while later in the day the pattern was reversed to accommodate the returning crowds. Falkirk Tryst was for many years the most important Scottish sale of black cattle, and was based at Stenhousemuir from 1785. Falkirk Tryst golf club now occupies most of the site.

This view was probably taken from the old town hall in Upper Newmarket Street looking north and probably dates from early 1906. The tram is passing the newly-built – but as yet unveiled statue – erected in memory of the fallen in the South African (Boer) War. This depicts a soldier from the Argyll and Sutherland Highlanders standing guard over the body of a wounded comrade, and was the work of John Archibald Campbell, a prolific architect who won many awards, including one for his design of the Queen Victoria Memorial School in Dunblane. Here the granite base is fresh, with the dedication panel yet to be fitted. The bronze statue itself is still covered. Behind is the distinctive burgh building which dates back to the 1870s. It has been described as Scots Baronial with a "… Frenchy truncated spire with iron cresting". It remains today as one of Falkirk's more recognisable structures, still in the care of the local council, and serves as the town centre management office. To the right of the statue is the YMCA building on the corner of Glebe Street.

Newmarket Street was formerly one large open expanse, but during the late nineteenth century the original Market Road was divided longitudinally into Upper and Lower Newmarket Streets, with a narrow terraced garden area between. Most of the lower area has been pedestrianised in recent times, while the upper length has served for many years as a departure point for local bus services – including the current Firstbus No. 11 circular service which has replaced and generally follows the former tram route. In this scene the statue still remains to be completed, and on the right is the bulk of the town hall. This was the former Corn Exchange of 1859 which was remodelled twenty years later at the extreme cost of £5,000,then ignominiously demolished in 1968 to much public disquiet. Its tower mimicked that across the street. The striking spire behind is that of the distinctive red sandstone St. Andrews West (formerly Falkirk Free Church) dating from 1896.

Looking back in a westward direction along the divide between the upper and lower parts of Newmarket Street. An underground gentleman's convenience was built below this end of the separating terrace – which had no connection to the Gentleman's Fountain at the opposite end of the thoroughfare! The town hall can be seen on the south side, while the façade on the right is little altered, although some of the shop fronts have been 'improved' over the years. The view is photographed from one of the buildings which then faced across the end of Newmarket Street. These were removed to allow for construction of Princes Street, opened in 1933 by the Prince of Wales (later to become the Duke of Windsor after abdicating his short reign as King Edward VIII). The bend into Vicar Street was initially of single track, and a signal lamp on the adjacent standard lit when another tram was approaching in the opposite direction, in an attempt to avoid confrontation!

Vicar Street leads north from the end of Newmarket Street, where if it was running today the tram would find that it was fighting a losing battle against the onrush of traffic heading in the opposite direction down a one way street! The buildings from this side of the tall tenement on the right were all swept away in the formation of Princes Street, the corner now occupied by the most incongruous half-timbered 'Tudor House' built in 1934. Whoever thought it was a fine idea to plonk a mock English Elizabethan structure in the middle of 1930s Falkirk may have been delusional. Most of the local street urchins seem to have gathered to add their presence to the photograph.

The same tenement accommodated the entrance to Falkirk's Grand Theatre, opened in 1903, but which was transformed in the 1930s to the Regal Cinema, with a new imposing frontage on to Princes Street.

Car No. 18 prepares to turn from Vicar Street into Newmarket Street under the watchful eye of one of the local constabulary. The entrance to the Grand Theatre, which was actually located behind the imposing tenement on the right can be seen – and can still be found to this day, although it probably now has a use only as an emergency exit from the Regal (now ABC) Cinema. The theatre sign is visible at first floor level, but the entrance was later made more apparent with a large canopy over the footpath. Next to the theatre entrance is 'Sweeney's Hairdressing Salon', an unfortunate (or intentional?) choice of name for an establishment of that profession! Above the head of the tram driver, the number '4' indicates the service number. Three cars, service Nos. 1, 3 and 5 ran the regular anticlockwise frequency, while Nos. 2, 4 and 6 did the clockwise circuit. The drivers knew at which passing place they were supposed to meet. Cars between Larbert and Camelon via Stenhousemuir had service numbers 7 and above and were known as the 'jerkers' – going back and forth rather than round and round!

Looking south up Vicar Street; on the left, all the buildings closer to the camera than Weir Street have been swept

away to give space for a traffic roundabout on what constitutes Falkirk's inner ring route leading from Garrison Place over to Park Street. The railway bridge here at Grahamston Station replaced an earlier level crossing which was superseded by a road diversion over a narrow bridge to the east. This also eventually was replaced when the tramway was built. The fanciful building created for the British Linen Bank in 1899 can be seen, and still exists, as do all of the buildings on the west side of the street. The tram is on the single line which led round into Lower Newmarket Street on the right.

Grahams Road looking north showing the mostly nineteenth century 'ribbon development' which made the entire (or virtually entire) circular route an obvious candidate for a tramway. Large numbers of artisans' houses were built in the one-time villages surrounding Falkirk, providing dwellings for the numerous workers attracted by employment in the newly-established iron works and associated industries. Many of these buildings have been removed in recent years, either leaving unsightly gap sites or replaced by more modern intrusions. The distinctive three storey tenement building on the left still stands today, but the single-storey shops beyond have been removed to widen the Meeks Road junction. The entire right side of the street as seen here has been swept away with, at the bend of the road in the distance, the roundabout giving access to the massive Central Retail Park, about which the best thing that can be said is that it *is* central, thus not dragging retail commerce and shoppers to some distant semi-rural suburb thus signalling the death-knell of the town centre as a shopping focus.

Journeying further north along Grahams Road on our anti-clockwise tram trip, we are here at the junction with Western Avenue on the left. The distinctive building on the far corner is the Oddfellows Hall which also remains today complete with a frieze inscription 'Loyal – Sir John De Graeme - Lodge'. No longer serving its built purpose, it now proclaims itself as the 'Megazone Falkirk Laser Game Centre'. The original entrance to the hall has a bearded head carved on to the key stone of the arch above the door – perhaps a sign from the original occupiers. The Oddfellows Society is one of several such friendly societies (in this case dating back to 1810, although the roots of the organisation stretch back into antiquity) which grew from medieval guilds, but the Oddfellows (Odd Fellows in the USA) were people without specific trade affiliations. Their Grahamston Hall was designed by James Strang, the building dating from 1882.

Further along Grahams Road, the streetscape here has changed remarkably little in the course of over 100 years. The buildings on both sides of the street remain little altered, only the nature of the businesses conducted showing modernisation; from haberdashery and greengrocers to carpet saleroom and beauty salon, but fortunately the nucleus of necessary local newsagent and the like has survived. The wide footpath also remains, but in keeping with many other parts of the burgh, now displays attractive flower beds. Along Gowan Avenue (next on the left) could be found Grahamston Ironworks, a major local employer until 1994, and home of the remarkable decorative cast iron gates which had been made in the works for the Edinburgh International Exhibition of 1886. After the last remnant of these works was demolished, the gates were saved for posterity and in 2002 dismantled, carefully refurbished and then re-erected by Carron Phoenix Ltd.

Tram No. 18, heading south along Grahams Road, having just crossed the canal bridge. John Street and the lanes on the left all led to wharfs on the canal bank. Of all the buildings in the scene, the only one remaining is that in the far distance, beyond the canal bridge, the old 'Red Lion Inn' which now has a life as a car hire office. The short row of houses on the left contained no less than three public houses. In the nineteenth century this area was home to several brick works and clay pits – the seams having been uncovered during construction of the canal at the end of the previous century. The tram is approaching Dalderse Avenue on the right, considered at one time to have been the site of the Battle of Falkirk in 1298 when King Edward of England roundly defeated the Scots' army of William Wallace. More recent consideration, however, puts the locus of the battle near to Hallglen on the other side of Falkirk.

Bainsford Bridge over the Forth & Clyde Canal, seen in the winter of 1905-1906, shortly after its reconstruction to carry electric trams. The cause of the argument with the Caledonian Railway Company, the position of the poles necessary to carry the overhead wire electric conductor for the tramway, can be seen here as evidence of an issue yet to be resolved. The poles remain in the 'as constructed' position, which the railway company correctly claimed fouled the use of the tow path for barge haulage ropes. One of the electric trams can just be discerned on the far side of the bridge, waiting for passengers who have had to walk the short, inconvenient, distance across the waterway. On the canal, just a few yards west of the bridge was Bainsford Basin, much used for despatch of cast iron products from the Carron Works, and the terminus of their dedicated waggonway connection to the works.

In this scene, the driver of tram No. 5 appears to be 'pushing his luck' by taking his car on to the canal bridge before the alteration had been made to the position of the offending overhead support poles. Not only that, but the destination displays 'Circular', although theoretically at this time the service operated as two distinct parts, either side of the two bridges. The Red Lion was then fulfilling its designated role as a public house, possibly having served as such since the time of construction of the canal.

By the middle of March 1906 the dispute with the railway company had been resolved and the new, cantilevered supports had been constructed. Only then would the owning company permit trams to cross the two bridges and complete the planned circular route. On each crossing the conductor had to go to the top deck and hold the trolley rope, in case of any potential for dewirement where the two sections of overhead met. With the canal's towing path on the north side of the

waterway, the new arrangement was made there, on the Bainsford side of the gap. The woman on the right, her image unknowingly preserved for posterity, indicates clearly the style of dress of the local female workers – shawl over the head and tightly grasped at the neck. She is passing a lurid Caledonian Railway poster extolling the pleasures to be found at Bridge of Allan – a destination unlikely to appeal greatly to this particular passer-by.

French-built tram No. 12 is given the signal that all is clear for it to proceed to cross the canal. A railway style semaphore signal indicated that the bridge was in the roadway state; it was raised horizontally if the bridge was in use for canal traffic. Not only this, but also points were built into the track to divert any tram which was not stopped in adequate time. Other than the former 'Red Lion' little remains of the nineteenth century buildings seen here. Everything on the far (west) side of the Bainsford Main Street has been demolished – replaced by the warehouse architecture style showrooms of 'Britain's Bedding Specialist'.

Main Street Bainsford is transformed into Carron Road here, at its junction with David's Loan and Mungalhead Road. This 1905 view has the latter road on the right, so the scene is looking south towards Falkirk. The Carron Company's waggonway formerly crossed just to the right of this scene, and ran immediately behind this row of houses which pre-dated it. Waggon Road on the former track indicates the original route of the line, and locally this is still known as the 'Waggonway' or 'Back Waggon'. On the left the red sandstone block which was home to the Cross Roads Inn on David's Loan still stands – although now without the benifit of the old pub – while all the old single storey workers' houses on the right have been removed. A recent survey opined that the *late nineteenth and twentieth century architecture* [of Bainsford] *is generally unappealing*. This could certainly be applied to the block which replaced these old cottages – it will meet today's sanitary requirements – which these would not.

Almost none of the nineteenth century dwellings which lined Carron Road have survived. Those built as ribbon development along the road – and the lesser groups of minimal standards workers' housing – were swept away before the end of the twentieth century to be replaced by the ubiquitous Lidl and Co-op complexes and associated modern housing developments. Basic housing for workers at the Carron – and other – foundries was generally of relatively poor standard by modern criteria but the three storey red sandstone tenements which line the east side of Carron Road north and south of Millflats Street were judged to be fit for modernisation, and were reconstructed internally in the 1980s. At the point where this scene was recorded, the two storey block on the right has been demolished to permit construction of the new 'bypass' of Dovecothall Street. Carron Road now ends here, the continuation of the old road bearing to the left now named Corran Avenue. Whose strange idea was the artificial transposition of the two vowels of the historic name into something meaningless? The single storey cottages alongside the tram still survive, with the Carronbridge Inn (The Soo Hoose) ending the block. Formerly it was matched by the Carronlodge Inn on the opposite side of the road, but in its place has recently been constructed the incongruously named Park Road development.

The new bridge over the River Carron, constructed for the tramway. This 1905 structure has stood the test of time, although now most through traffic is diverted on to Dovecothall Street. Just further to the left there was formerly a bridge over a short canal which led from the navigable River Carron right into the iron works, with a loading basin from which iron products could be despatched. A further harbour, Carronshore, was developed downstream, which was also connected to the iron works by way of the extensive private waggonway. This was converted in the 1860s to a standard gauge railway, but always remained the property of the company.

The works developed considerably during the Victorian era, and an imposing new frontage was built running along the perimeter of the works, on the west side of Carron Road. Originally the road (and the parallel waggonway) had taken off in a north-westerly direction after the Carron canal crossing, but the new façade caused a diversion to require the road to take a right-angled bend round the extended perimeter of the works. As soon as the tramway was operational, arrangements were put in place for provision of workers' special cars at shift times. Normally two cars went off in a clockwise direction, another two heading the opposite way. The first workers' specials are shown here, the cars still bright and shiny. Pressure on space was so great that every hand hold was latched on to, and the fenders of the cars were an obvious ledge to stand on for a free hurl. Very soon sloping metal guards were fitted to prevent – or at least make more difficult – this practice.

The sharp bend at the works' corner was of single track, hence conductors were required to ensure no car was approaching from the opposite direction. The obvious solution of erecting signals seems never to have been adopted. The north gate to the works was also a railway level crossing with the line leading to several of the company's collieries, and to Carronshore Dock. It could be busy, and a cause of frequent interruption to the tramway timetables. Little sign of the original works remains today. The iron works site is still in industrial use, part utilised by Carron Phoenix Ltd, makers of stainless steel pressings, mostly domestic sink units. A sad reminder of the former status is the preservation of the former entrance to the works – isolated and a symbol of former glory.

The Carron Company purchased their first locomotive for use about the works in 1861 and eventually owned sixteen, used on the company's extensive internal works system and also at their various collieries. This is their second locomotive, its Carron number can just be made out on the side of the boiler. The old machine was a regular on the lines in and around the works until it was scrapped in 1936. A similar old locomotive also by Hawthorn of Leith is a prized exhibit in the Royal Museum of Scotland in Edinburgh.

After winding its way through the undeveloped area from Carron by Goshen the next settlement reached was Stenhousemuir. This part of the route would generate little traffic, with (then) only a small cluster of cottages at Goshen. Near here had been the ancient monument known as Arthur's O'on. Its function can never now be investigated since it was torn down in 1743, the dressed masonry being taken away to repair a nearby weir. It had been described as the most

complete Roman structure in Britain before this remarkable piece of vandalism by the local laird. Strangely, a supposedly accurate replica of the structure was built to serve as a dovecote on the roof of the stables of Penicuik House in Midlothian in 1763. Stenhousemuir was a small collection of cottages until the meeting place for the cattle sales or 'trysts' was moved here from Roughcastle in 1785. Held on the first Tuesdays of August, September and October, cattle gathered at the 200 acre tryst field from all over Scotland. Temporary dwellings, tents and the like gave shelter to the hundreds of drovers, while it was estimated that over 150,000 head of cattle and sheep changed hands anually. Much of the site of the tryst is now in use as the renowned Falkirk Tryst Golf Course.

The Plough Hotel in Stenhousemuir still occupies its prominent position between Main Street on the right and King Street on the left. Main Street here no longer has its former importance, and with the new shopping centre and associated parking facilities it is no longer the 'main' route east to west. Tryst Road leads off to the left. The works of the famous Andrew McCowan toffee maker (the Special Highland Toffee, with the trademark Highland Cow has possibly given dentists more fillings to replace than the makers would wish to advertise) are built on part of the tryst grounds. The toffee maker, with a history stretching back to the early years of the twentieth century went into liquidation after about 100 years of trading, but has amalgamated with Millar Confectionary and has traded as New McCowan Ltd since 2006 still producing Highland Toffee.

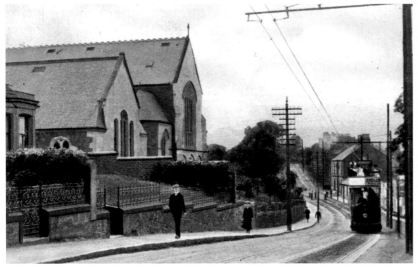

Burnhead Brae between Stenhousemuir and Larbert, photographed looking west. The actual boundary between the two villages was at the Broomage Burn, which ran below the road at the lowest point of the dip. On the left side of the road stands Larbert West Church of Scotland, although the front retaining wall is now considerably higher – a slice of the bank in front of the church having been shaved off when the road was widened in the 1920s. It was built in 1901 as the United Free Church of Larbert. Opposite is ground which was not built upon until a garage, filling station and caravan sales depot were created.

In the early days of tramway operation car No. 6 was photographed in Larbert Main Street, waiting to return the short distance to the car sheds in Stirling Road. The scene, looking west as seen here from Larbert Cross has been radically altered in recent years, with all buildings on the west side of Stirling Road removed to permit construction of the new diversionary road. The left (south) side of the street here, along with the Red Lion on the right hand corner, are unchanged. It is difficult today to imagine an electric tramway threading through these narrow streets. The red sandstone tenement on the left which itself replaced the former Wheat Sheaf Inn at that time had shops at street level; these are now gone although the building remains.

Probably recorded in the period shortly after the end of the First World War, this scene records the nature of Falkirk Road, Larbert prior to its reconstruction to accommodate tramway improvements. At this time it was the the main highway from the central lowlands of Scotland to Stirling and the north. Despite the supervising presence of the bulk of the 1820 built Larbert Old Church, every building on the left (west) side of the street has now gone. From the Railway Tavern on the extreme left, past the original post office, nothing remains. This stretch of road still exists but is by-passed for through traffic, hence is possibly now as quiet as it was prior to construction of the tramway more than 100 years ago.

A tramcar on the clockwise circle passes across the original Larbert Bridge over the River Carron, immediately after opening of the tramway service. Closest to the camera is the arch spanning the Carron Works lade which then ran parallel to the river for some distance and was the major supply of fresh water for all processes at the Ironworks. The closeness to the line of the Antonine Roman wall and to another Roman road just a short distance upstream has led to speculation that there was a Roman bridge across the Carron. The 'old' bridge was built in 1782 and has withstood centuries of the river in spate; however its narrow width was an impediment for road traffic and a new, wider, concrete arch was built downstream in 1926. Tolls were formerly charged on the original bridge, payable to the Earl of Callendar and Linlithgow … *four pennies Scots for each cart … and twelve pennies Scots for each score of droves of cows*. One pound Scots was rated as one twelfth of the pound Sterling.

The Electric Car at Larbert Arches is the title of this postcard, probably taken before the line was officially opened for public use. The driver is without uniform, suggesting that this is a scene during initial trial operation. Behind the tram can be seen the fourteen arched railway viaduct constructed for the Scottish Central Railway in 1848. It was the scene of a spectacular accident nineteen years later when a southbound cattle train derailed, with some of the wagons and their unfortunate contents hurled to the ground below. The tramway threaded its way beneath the northmost arch of the viaduct; the clearance so tight that the Board of Trade's inspector required the tramway company to erect boards telling passengers not to touch the wires! These were fitted to the sides of the bridge and remained for decades after the last open-topped tram had passed below. They have been removed only in recent years.

This rural scene by the old corn mill on Larbert Road completes the trip around the circular route. The depot structure, always known as the 'Cars Sheds', was located just behind the photographer. While the circular route was the first one to be built, in these early days of enthusiasm for trams as the up-to-date and preferred means of urban transport, thoughts very quickly turned to expansion. Plans were prepared for further lines to serve Grangemouth and Laurieston. The circular line in its first complete year of operation carried no less than 3,548,473 passengers, so the omens for the success of the other lines appeared positive.

Parliamentary authority for both extensions was obtained in 1906 (subsequently varied the following year), and after some strenuous opposition and hard negotiation with Mr Forbes of Callendar Estate, construction commenced. Forbes confessed to being in favour of the tram proposals in principle, but wanted them (so far as was possible) not to be visible from his estate. The Earl of Zetland, proprietor of much of the land around Grangemouth, also raised objections, but these were mostly overcome when road widening schemes were agreed. Construction of the first planned extension, that to Laurieston village, some one and a half miles east of Falkirk was commenced in June 1909 and was completed within three months. Because of the narrow nature of the west end of the High Street, trams only used this length when coming from, or returning to, the Car Sheds. The Laurieston route was therefore run as a separate entity with no through running on to the circular route. The terminus for these cars was in High Street, at the top of Kirk Wynd and just west of Falkirk's famous steeple.

Looking in the opposite (westerly) direction, this tram waiting to start for Laurieston is standing at the top of Kirk Wynd, the streetscape having altered (architecturally at least) remarkably little in the century since then. Pedestrianised entirely from end to end since 1990, High Street is still a major shopping centre, despite the plethora of retail centres which have been built in recent years to satisfy rampant consumerism (in which way Falkirk differs little from most comparable conurbations). The Railway Hotel's red sandstone building was only about ten years old when this photo was taken, and is unchanged, although now occupied by Burton's menswear with an added "modern" shop front. The remarkable pointed turret has been likened to a witch's hat! On the south side of the street the building with the twin pediment alongside the tram remains, but everything to the east (towards the camera) has been reconstructed recently to form the entrance to the Howgate Shopping Centre.

Looking west along the narrow eastern end of High Street with a tram heading for Laurieston. East Bridge Street takes off here on the left, and remains, but the entire north side of this area was razed to the ground in the early 1960s to allow construction of the unpopular Callendar Riggs Shopping Centre. So unsatisfactorily did this development sit in this space that it in turn was flattened after just over twenty years' use, eventually to be replaced in 1992 after some time by the (slightly) more aesthetically pleasing and commercially  more viable Callendar Square development. Lost in the process was Silver Row, with its historic public house, The Masonic Arms, said to have been visited by Robert Burns in 1787. Also in this scene, just beyond the horse and cart standing beside the tram is Burnhead Lane, on the corner of which is the Cross Keys Inn – where Burns spent the night of 25th August during the same visit. On his attic bedroom window the bard, using a diamond, inscribed four lines of poetry. The Cross Keys also closed in the 1960s, but the window pane has been preserved and can be found today at the Burns National Heritage Park at Alloway.

Cyclists share the road with the distant tramcar on Callendar Road, in this 1910 postcard photograph. The scene is recorded with the lodge and entrance gates leading to Bellmount House (of which nothing remains – the site now covered by a car park) on the north side of the road, while on the right is the wall behind which was the town's first gas works (of 1830), entered from Corporation Street. Further on the right, after the road junction, and the area now occupied by a traffic roundabout to Bellevue Street, lay the ancient Marion's Well, latterly used as an open air public laundry. Beyond that on the south side of the main road followed the high boundary wall of Callendar Park estate, now in the care of the local authority, a splendidly kept resource for all to appreciate. The Callendar Road to Laurieston was built on this alignment in 1829.

Further east along Callendar Road, with a solitary tram giving a free pull to a cyclist who is hanging on to the platform pole. The service between Falkirk and Laurieston normally utilised one tramcar only, giving a twenty minute frequency for a fare of 1½d. In order to minimise costs, the track was not laid on concrete, as would be normal, but constructed on sleepers – this economy was to cause problems later on. The otherwise deserted road is bounded to the right (south) by the high wall enclosing the estate of Forbes of Callendar House. The Forbes family came into the estate after the previous lairds, the Livingstones, made a major

political blunder by supporting the wrong side during the Jacobite insurgencies of 1715 and 1745, their misjudgements resulting in their estates being forfeited. Behind the wall on the right is to be found one of the best-preserved lengths of the Roman Wall, within Callendar Park. Forbes insisted that the tramway be constructed on the north side of the road, as far as he could require from his property. Beyond the tram, on the left is now the entrance to the new Graeme High School, which opened for its first pupils in August 2000.

To pass below the skew bridge carrying the Stirlingshire Midland Junction Railway (which even before opening in 1850 was absorbed by the Edinburgh & Glasgow Railway, then became part of the North British Railway from 1865) it was necessary to lower the road surface to provide adequate clearance. This was done as shown, with the road dropped by nearly three feet. The resulting 'dropped' road level persists to this day – but how many of the thousands of vehicle drivers who use it today realise that the Falkirk tramcars were responsible?

Looking west towards Falkirk from Laurieston's Toll Brae. With the distinctive railway bridge in the background, the scene is instantly recognisable today, although the old houses have all gone, and the area is now dominated by a massive road traffic roundabout. The village of Laurieston was a planned settlement, laid out from 1756 by

the then laird, Francis Lord Napier who gave it the name 'New Merchiston' from his family seat in Edinburgh. The land and the new village were then sold at the end of 1762 to Sir Lawrence Dundas – who promptly changed the name to Lawrencetown which through time became Laurieston. Although home to the cottage industries of hand-loom weaving and nail-making, the advent of the tramway allowed the inhabitants to travel in to Falkirk for alternative employment.

This is the Laurieston scene looking east towards the tramway terminus at Mary Square in the centre of the village. Authority had in fact been given to extend the line a further half mile to the far end of the built-up area towards Polmont, but this was never constructed. It can be seen that, having passed below the skew bridge, and out of sight of Mr. Forbes, the track has taken what would be the normally accepted position in the centre of the main road. Grahamsdyke Street leading off to the left runs parallel to, and just to the south, of the line of the Antonine Wall. The name Graham's Dyke is said to have derived from the Old Scots for 'strong wall'.

3rd September 1909 can be confidently stated to be the date of this scene in Mary Square, Laurieston as this is the official photograph taken at the opening of the tramway extension. The inspection for the Board of Trade had just been completed and operation commenced immediately thereafter. The tramway manager, by now Mr. Douglas Hays, is the gent wearing the straw hat and standing in front of the stair of car 10, with Chief Inspector Ronaldson the smart uniformed figure between the cars. Other dignitaries include members of Falkirk Town Council. It will be noted that the car on the left (No. 18) now has a top deck cover fitted. The Laurieston section was run strictly to timetable, unlike the circular route, where schedules were subject to frequent disruption by operation of the two canal swing bridges which closed the roadway to all traffic, including the trams.

The two cars carrying the participants in the opening ceremony are seen here setting off on the return to Falkirk. Car 18's top deck cover significantly increased the benefit provided during inclement weather. Douglas Hays had intended to have these fitted to all of the eighteen cars, but on examination it was discovered that the French-built cars, after only three years in operation, were exhibiting severe signs of the bad workmanship and poor materials used in their construction. Already considerable expense had been incurred to keep these vehicles operational. As a consequence only three cars were considered structurally sound

enough to carry the additional weight, the English-built cars, Nos. 16, 17 and 18. The top decks were fitted in March 1908, and to allow the cars to pass below the Camelon railway bridges the roadway was lowered, the cost involved being met by the Tramway Company.

Car 18 is waiting in Falkirk's High Street by the Steeple to commence its short journey to Laurieston. Forming the focal point of the town centre, the Steeple was built in 1814 to replace the original which was attached to the Tolbooth and dated from 1697. This part of the High Street still remains as the major gathering point and is now completely pedestrianised. No explanation has been obtained for the unusually large gathering of young men.

In its top covered state, car 17 makes its way along Main Street, Larbert – a scene now greatly changed. The long three storey terrace (Stewartfield Buildings) with the distinctive turreted corner on Victoria Road has completely disappeared, replaced by four blocks of modern flats, set in attractively landscaped and wooded surroundings. The top covers for the three trams only lasted until about 1913. They were taken off and passed to the Dumbarton Tramway Company in the west of Scotland.

Car 18 in as built condition, before fitting with the top cover, with Chief Inspector Ronaldson standing on the front step. This scene is in Newmarket Street, in front of Falkirk's statue in honour of the Duke of Wellington, the work of Robert Forrest. First positioned in 1854 in High Street beside the steeple it was moved to this spot in 1905, not long before this photograph was taken. The statue is now surrounded by attractive flower beds.

Detail of the covered top fitted to the three English cars is well shown in this photograph, taken at Larbert Station. The top covers were supplied by Hurst Nelson & Company of Motherwell. At 6ft 1ins headroom inside they were higher than many such cars used on other systems. The car is standing on the railway bridge, with the station off to the right. Behind can be seen the distinctive four storey Station Terrace built *circa* 1900 by the Moscardini brothers in expectation of Larbert's position on the railway network making it the 'Crewe of Scotland'. Their venture was not the success they anticipated and the building remained for years as a monument to their unfulfilled ambitions. The building *does* still remain – just. About 25 years ago the upper storeys were removed and a new mansard roof was built on the now much lower structure. All that really remains to indicate that what now stands still incorporates part of the original are the (now modernised) shop fronts with the two distinctive pediments, one gracing each elevation.

Car 17 has by this stage lost its top deck cover. Photographed in Larbert Road near the car sheds this is from the time of the First World War or immediately thereafter. The demands of the recruiting sergeant reduced dramatically the numbers of men fit and able to work on the trams, and the first women to work as 'lady conductors' were employed in June 1915. A year later the first women tram drivers were appointed – said to be the first such in Scotland. The Falkirk line was considered to be 'suitable' for the fair sex's ability to be trained as tramcar drivers, having no major gradients to cope with. The driver here is W Ronaldson and the conductress Mrs Kerr; an entry in the staff discipline book for 27th June 1917 records that Conductress Kerr was given a caution "for playing about in the road with her driver"!

French-built car No. 2 was photographed about the same period, and about the same location, with driver Tom Fraser and conductress Maggie Penman. Alterations made to these cars can be seen: all of the original trucks were replaced by new ones supplied by Hurst Nelson as early as 1908, additional ventilation was provided by an adaptation of the top of the central window; the original dash plates were replaced by a new, lower ones, also from Hurst Nelson, this change commencing in 1916 as the originals had rusted through; new stairs were also provided. The car was fitted with steel protection over the fenders to prevent free rides being gained by people hanging from its rear.

In the years immediately preceding the First World War viable petrol engined motor buses appeared on the local scene, with one – possibly owned by either James Campbell or Robert Taylor (both from Bannockburn) being used to run a one-off service to the Falkirk Tryst in Stenhousemuir in September 1910. A certain Walter Alexander of Brown Street, Camelon, claimed to be the first 'Falkirk Bairn' to avail himself of the new opportunity. He may have been the first to operate a regular and timetabled service – to and from Bonnybridge at weekends only after July 1914, but he was pipped to the post by the Falkirk Tramway's manager. Through the next fifty years the Alexander name became synonymous for the Scottish bus industry in its many manifest guises. Despite his assertions, Alexander was not the first to operate motor buses in the town – that distinction belonged to the Falkirk District Motor Car Company more than ten years earlier. For the Tramway Company Douglas Hays was quick to rise to the opportunity presented by reliable motor buses, particularly as his directors had decided that they would not build the authorised tramway from Falkirk to Grangemouth. This had been delayed by protracted negotiations and was, with the benifit of hindsight, probably the best decision in the light of future progress. Hays purchased the company's first charabanc, a Commer registered LN9772, in June 1913, more than a year before Alexander's purchase of his Belhaven. The first Commer is seen here on a hire, along with the second vehicle, another Commer, MS 1176. These were actively promoted as the 'Grey Torpedo Cars' in direct competition with Alexander's 'Royal Blue' branding. The drivers of these two charabancs are John Chalmers on number 2 on the left, with David Millar in charge of number 1 on the right.

Tram and bus operations were considerably affected by the First World War. War industries brought scores of additional workers to the area, but lack of manpower for maintenance brought problems of a different nature.

Touring continued during the early months of the war and attempts were made to operate services to take workers to and from the various local war related manufactories. By 1919, when Walter Alexander bought his fourth vehicle, the Tramway Company was operating no less than 22 buses and charabancs and was thus by far the premier operator in the area, with regular routes to Grangemouth and Bo'ness. Garage accommodation was provided on the ground beside the original car sheds in Larbert Road – the benefits of the spacious site originally purchased being fully utilised. This 1919 view shows tram and bus together, the latter with a large canvas 'gas-bag' in a wooden enclosure on the roof. During the war, many buses were converted to use town's gas as fuel.

FALKIRK AND DISTRICT TRAMWAYS COMPANY, LTD.

MOTOR TOURS.

EVER since their commencement in June of this year the demand for our Public Motor Tours has been exceedingly gratifying, not only on account of the financial aspect of the business, but as showing that we have supplied a very real want. In this period of great unrest and disturbance many no doubt have been obliged to curtail, or even forego, their usual summer holiday, and in consequence are only too thankful to have facilities placed at their disposal whereby a brief respite can be snatched from the cares and worries of everyday life.

For thorough rest and relaxation there is nothing more pleasurable or health-giving than a Motor Run, and that this fact has been realised is proved by the great popularity of our Public Tours. If you have not already participated in these, do not fail to take advantage of one at least of the following Excursions which will be run during week commencing Monday, August 16th:—

MONDAY, August 16th.

BLACKNESS.—Leave Newmarket Street 6.30 p.m. Arrive back about 9.30 p.m. Fare, 1/6.

TUESDAY, August 17th.

CAMPSIE GLEN.—Leave Newmarket Street 3 p.m. Arrive back about 9.30 p.m. Fare, 2/3.

WEDNESDAY, August 18th.

LOCH LOMOND, *via* Killearn and Balloch.—Leave Newmarket Street 2.30 p.m. Arrive back about 9.30 p.m. Fare, 4/9.

THURSDAY, August 19th.

ABERFOYLE, *via* Stirling and Port of Menteith.—Leave Newmarket St. 2.30 p.m. Arrive back about 9 p.m. Fare, 4/-.

FRIDAY, August 20th.

BLACKNESS.—Leave Newmarket Street 6.30 p.m. Arrive back about 9.30 p.m. Fare, 1/6.

Seats may be booked at John Callander's, High Street, Falkirk. (Tel. 68).

Tour advertisement from August 1915.

Heading the line up of Tramway Company charabancs on a large private hire is Tilling-Stevens MS2021 purchased in March 1919, with standing to the right its driver David Millar. The Tilling-Stevens petrol electric engine became the prime mover of choice for many years, said to be the consequence of the incorporation of electric drive familiar to the tramway based employees. It was also surprisingly economical, and many of these vehicles saw highly profitable use after withdrawal from revenue service when sold on to showmen for use supplying power to sideshows. The omnibus side of the business was taking off at such speed that the directors decided to float an entirely new company to concentrate on this element. This came into being in December 1919, the Tramway Company's fleet of 22 buses (all Tilling-Stevens except the one original Commer) then being transferred to the new Scottish General Omnibus Company Limited.

A 1919 record of the Falkirk Tramway Company's bus fleet at the time of formation of the Scottish General Omnibus Company. The line-up outside the depot consists of Tilling-Stevens – some with the gas bag container on the roof – plus, closest to the camera the solitary Commer. Unfortunately the original glass plate negative has been damaged, but the scene is worth including for its historical relevance.

In July 1920 Walter Alexander took his wife – plus a selection of Falkirk's senior 'Bairns' and their wives on a ground-breaking and probably extremely arduous and uncomfortable 560 miles round trip to John O'Groats and back – definitely not for the faint-hearted! This was supposedly the first occasion that a charabanc party had reached this extremity of the Scottish mainland. The ensuing publicity did Walter Alexander's business no harm whatsoever. The party were duly photographed outside the John O'Groats Hotel – which at least in 1920 appears to have been open for trade –

something missing today. Described by a fairly recent perceptive visitor as a 'tartan hued dump', the area vies in awfulness with the tackiness of the "visitor attraction" at the opposite end of the British Isles – Land's End (which mercifully is spared the tartan element). The trip was a good advert for the reliability of the Leyland-engined charabanc. This was purchased after the end of the war, ex-R.A.F. It took both the registration number (MS 1723) and the 27-seat body from Alexander's second Belhaven purchased in 1916.

Typical of the many Tilling-Stevens petrol-electric buses was this, No. 50 in the fleet, MS 4063 dating from 1922. The view was taken for the body builder, F D Cowieson of St Rollox in Glasgow. This company, founded in 1907 to manufacture prefabricated steel buildings (an idea half a century in advance of necessity), soon diversified into other areas, including bus bodies – manufacturing many for Glasgow Corporation. At the end of 1922, the highest number in the fleet of vehicles owned by Walter Alexander was 15, again emphasising how the tail came to wag the dog when the Alexander name was chosen to adorn the sides of most of Scotland's buses after the 1930s.

Near Carron Dams, the road was fully occupied by the double track tramway. The road was necessarily closed to all traffic. When the reconstruction process was complete, the road and the area occupied by the tram track were surfaced with tar macadam, giving a most superior finish and smooth ride – not just to the trams, but to all other

road traffic, including competing bus traffic. When the reconstruction was complete, the Tramway Company applied for a provisional order to give them sole rights to provide the required passenger service round the circle. The suggestion did not find favour and this part of the provisional order was unceremoniously rejected. This is Stenhouse Road at what is now Lodge Drive. Stenhouse Lodge at the entrance to the eponymous estate has gone as indeed has the mansion house itself. Dating in parts from 1622, and the home in the eighteenth century of Sir Michael Bruce (destroyer of Arthur's O'on), its listed status did not save it from demolition in the 1960s.

Carron Road photographed after completion of the renewal of the tramway infrastructure. Comparison with the scene as depicted on page 6 which is taken just a few yards further south than this, and twenty years earlier shows both differences and similarities. While at this point the track was always double, the proportion of single track was much reduced (from 67% to 25%) during the reconstruction. Why the opportunity was not seized then to make the entire circle of double track is unknown. The overhead has been renewed, with the original side bracket poles replaced by span wires. Behind looms the bulk of Carron Works, whose furnaces lit up the sky at night creating an appearance akin to Dante's Inferno – particularly when low cloud covered the site.

Motor bus competition abetted by rapidly disintegrating track led the tramway company to seek approval to abandon the short line to Laurieston. While it had served a useful purpose before the First World War, buses were seen as more able to run on to Polmont , or to serve more outlying settlements. However, the tram company, now a part of the Fife Tramway Light & Power Company was not allowed to atrophy and plans were put in motion to reconstruct the track of the highly profitable circular route to modern standards and provide a fleet of ultra modern trams to run on it. Agreement was reached with the local authorities involved, with work completed in 1927, much of the work attracting government grants for the alleviation of unemployment. This 1920s reconstruction scene is near Goshen at Carrongrange Avenue, now remarkably changed with on the left the entrance to the new Larbert High School, while all the old cottages have been replaced by smart modern bungalows. One immovable feature is the castellated spire of the McLaren Memorial Parish Church.

Looking back to the east on the same occasion and at the same location on Stenhouse Road, with the reinforced concrete foundation for the reconstructed tramway being poured. For most of the reconstruction, the road was completely closed to other traffic. Needless to say takings dropped significantly during the period of disruption, when the circle was run as a u-shape which varied as the construction phase moved round the route. On the left can be seen the mobile workshop, with a power connection hooked over the tramway overhead which, although there were no trams running here, was obviously still 'live'. All tramway ancillary equipment was suitable for direct current only.

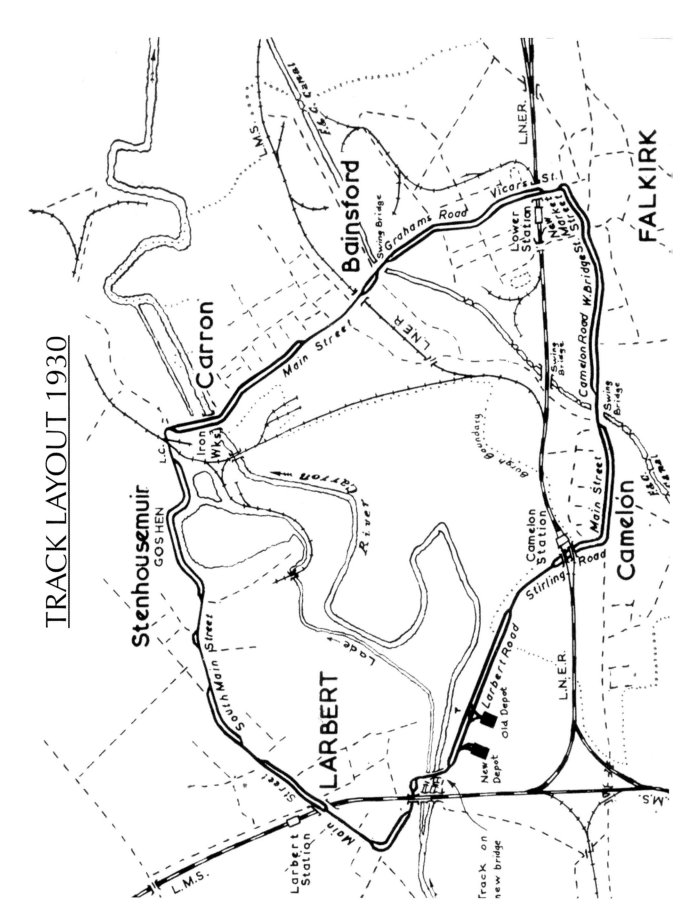

TRACK LAYOUT 1930

Reconstruction of the tramway along Larbert Road gave a fine well-paved highway to the north. The tram tracks were well founded on their new reinforced concrete base and the smooth road, the rails level with the surface raising no objection from drivers of motor traffic. Unemployment alleviation grants, when used in this manner ensured that there was a lasting benefit to the community (a message there somewhere for today's politicians?). The development of the transport facilities of the tramway and omnibus departments at this, their headquarters is well shown – the benefits of having commenced in a green field site apparent. One of the open-top trams is approaching, and the entrance to the original tram depot can be made out, now in the middle of the burgeoning complex.

In the workshops the facilities served both bus and tram. This carefully posed scene shows the maintenance team working on the engine of 1923 Tilling-Stevens bus MS 4558 (which also had bodywork by Cowieson). On the far side of the shop is a wheel lathe, used for work on tram wheels, which is driven by belting from overhead shafts. In front of the tram on the right are several pairs of wheels, including two which are totally shattered. If this accidentally happened while the tram was in service, it could only with difficulty be brought back to the depot. A low four wheeled jack would be inserted below the damaged element and the car towed back cautiously.

The basic starting point for the eventual Alexander bus empire is emphasised by these views of Walter Alexander's first petrol store house and the first bus garage behind the shop in Brown Street.

When the (very necessary) petrol safety regulations, deemed compulsory today are taken into consideration this wooden structure is on the basic side. Early buses not infrequently went on fire as a result of petrol spillage!

LIST OF TOURS

FOR SEASON 1925

BY

Alexanders' Royal Blue Coaches.

··

| GARAGE— | BOOKING OFFICE— |
| 'Phone **266.** | Phone **424.** |

··

W. ALEXANDER & SONS, Ltd.,

MOTOR ENGINEERS,

BROWN STREET, CAMELON.

GEO. INGLIS, PRINTER, FALKIRK.

Previous page: An idea of the complexities of running an organisation such as the ever-expanding General Bus Company is given by this glimpse of the stores. If it wasn't there, then the capacity to make it probably was! The benefits of fleet standardisation can be well appreciated, but while this aim was adhered to whenever possible, expansion meant that smaller companies absorbed brought into the fleet many strange and wonderful vehicles, including – from Peter Crerar of Crieff such exotic beasts as the Lancia, the Berliet and the De Dion (Crerar acted as agent for many makes and built many bodies on to imported chassis).

Another busy department at Larbert Road was the tyre fitters' corner. Inner tubes were fitted to all tyres then, and many tyres were allowed on the road in a condition which could not be contemplated today. 'Gaiters' were fitted over damaged covers, patches made on inner tubes and inside the tyres themselves. The device (a bead breaker) in the centre looks remarkably similar to that used by tyre fitters to this day.

It would appear that there was little cause to smile if you had your photograph taken when working for the tram or bus company. This is Chief Inspector Ronaldson and some of his senior staff (and his dog). David Millar is in the centre of the back row, but other names are unknown. Any assistance with identification would be greatly appreciated, please contact the author via the publisher.

'Cashing-in' was an essential part of every shift, with takings required to balance exactly against the number and value of tickets sold. 'Overs' were just as badly received by management as 'Shorts' and repeated discrepancies could lead to dismissal. On many tramways, female staff recruited during First World War manpower shortages were displaced as soon as possible by returning ex-servicemen. In Falkirk, however, the expansion of bus service provision resulted in most conducting duties being undertaken by women – both on bus and tram.

The travelling experience of intrepid passengers was improved radically with the change to pneumatic tyres which took place gradually *circa* 1926-7. The appearance of the vehicles changed also, the livery was simplified, and they assumed a more 'modern' guise. This Tilling-Stevens MS 4918 (fleet number 72, and also with a Cowieson body) was of 1924, but was not among those which passed into Alexander's control in June 1930. It is seen at the Grangemouth stance, *en route* to Maddiston via Laurieston and Brightons – a route which encompassed both planned tram extensions.

The red Thornycrofts operated by Hugh Pender presented a real challenge to the decaying trams – even if they were running on brand new track. That counted for nothing in the eyes and brains of the travelling public. Speed, comfort and modernity were deemed much more important. MS 7782 was purchased in December 1927. This photograph of King Street, Stenhousemuir probably dates from the following year. Pender operated a circular service over the tram route, but deviating here to pick up passengers off the tram's circle. The house wife on the left is 'stoning' her front step into a state of acceptable cleanliness. Of this scene only the memory now remains, nothing – other than the furthest building in the distance – still exists. Pender's business, which had started in January 1921 with a route to Maddiston which only lasted two years, then moved into tramway territory with a competing circular service. The firm retained its independence until January 1931 when it was – in theory – bought out by the Falkirk & District Traction Company. For a further five years it continued to trade under the Pender name, but was operated by Alexander on behalf of the Traction Company [matters became more than a little confused at this time of rapid change].

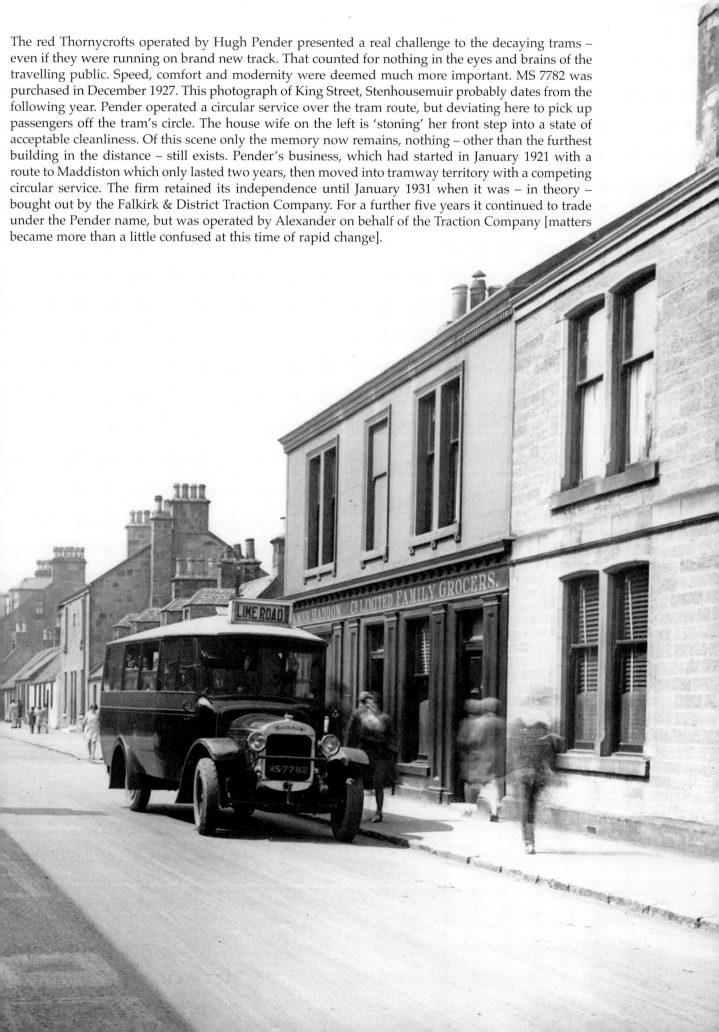

The first purpose-built 'bus station' in the district was constructed in Falkirk's Cow Wynd at Windhill Road in 1928, with the date built in to the top of the end of the structure. It was used solely by Wilson Marshall & Sons of Avonbridge for their services, which are delineated on the canopy. After use as the local social security office the premises are today occupied by Burnside Highland Dress, and with most indications of its original use now long gone; even the date has been removed from the pediment. Wilson Marshall, who traded under the 'Venture' name, was founded in 1919 operating from Falkirk to Avonbridge then on to Slamannan and eventually as far as Airdrie, while another route operated to Bathgate; the undertaking and some twenty vehicles – mostly Thornycrofts – were subsumed by Alexanders' in March 1930.

Fairly typical of the type of motor bus available – many operators taking them on hire-purchase – in the late 1920s was this 28 seat Albion obtained second-hand by Hugh Pender from J Connelly of Elderslie in 1929. Pender's business and his fleet of 22 buses nominally became a subsidiary of Alexanders' from 1st January 1931, but legal ownership was retained by the Tramway (now Traction) Company. This view, with driver Robert McLachlan and conductress Lottie Nimmo was recorded at Station Terrace, Larbert – the fish and chip shop then run by Mr. Santis.

Bowlers queue to board Alexander's bus MS4316, heading for Kilsyth. It was a May 1923 purchase; a Leyland with a Leyland-built 32 seat body which was numbered 18 in the fleet. This body was known by Leyland as the 'Edinburgh' style, having been supplied on vehicles sold to that corporation when the cable trams were being reconstructed for electric operation and buses were needed to operate temporary replacement services. The notice in the

window advertises the Dunipace and Denny Games, to be held on Saturday 18th August. As this date did not fall on a Saturday again until 1934, it can be fairly safely assumed that the photo dates from the year that the vehicle was delivered – also since the vehicle was withdrawn from service in 1926, the timescale becomes rather limited.

Word spread quickly that the new rails were to be graced by new trams – the consequence of which was that the standard of turn-out of the twenty-year old vehicles was allowed to deteriorate rapidly. Elderly tram No. 6 compares unfavourably with Pender's brand new bus heading off down King Street at the Point in Stenhousemuir. The brand new – state of the art – Albion bus (MS 8270 purchased in July 1928) typifies the competition which the very basic tram was up against. However, the tram company did not despair. A vast amount of capital had been poured into the tramway infrastructure and they were not about to throw in the towel. By this date, the tram was very shabby, its once gleaming Prussian blue paintwork now faded and worn, so much so that one observer thought the livery of the trams was 'grey'.

Tram 12 in 1929, just before it was withdrawn, seen in Larbert Road, outside the depot. The photographer had been told that a new fleet of modern trams was about to be delivered – and indeed, the first of the new cars was delivered just three weeks later. The opportunity for a record showing the old and the new side by side appears to have been missed however as none showing such a comparison has been seen.

In August 1929 the first of the new 'Pullman' trams was delivered to the car sheds, and after assembly in the old depot was placed in service on the 28th of that month. Of the first delivery of four cars, No. 3 was the first to be placed in service, and was photographed for posterity in Larbert Road. The contrast with the original fleet of dilapidated four wheel originals could not have been greater, with a new livery of bright red adopted. The ultra modern vehicle exemplified the latest tramway technology, and was more than equal to the motor bus of the day. The smooth quiet ride of the Pullman tram on the new track could only invite comparisons with the newest of the local buses, which were however only as comfortable as the road surface, passed through the suspension, permitted. Unfortunately the very best of road surfaces was along the tram route – to which the many competing buses contributed nothing. The bill in the near window of the new tram advertises the carnival to be held in Falkirk Town Hall in the first week of October.

The new trams incorporated many novel features utilising the very latest technology. One of the most unusual was the manner in which the traction motors were mounted – longitudinally, rather than the more normal transverse fitting, with the drive to the axles being by worm gears. This arrangement, allied to the use of roller bearings throughout gave the new cars remarkably smooth and very quiet operation. However, the passenger was more likely to note and appreciate the comfortable cushioned seating, which in the first ten cars was longitudinally arranged down the sides of the car – but each of the seats was formed individually – no more the slide along polished wooden seats when the motorman applied the brake suddenly! Each of the new cars cost almost £1,900, a sum now equivelant to £365,000 if based upon the relative value of average earnings.

Although the peak years of the postcard industry were past, the new trams were photographed to bring old scenes up to date. Not only is the tram (No. 2) new to this scene, but the bridge over the River Carron is also a replacement for the old arch (which still remains just upstream). When the road was reconstructed in 1925-6, a reinforced concrete arch bridge was constructed on an alignment to the east of the old. Trams used this from the middle of June 1926. For some unknown reason this track was laid single – providing double lines would have incurred little additional cost and simplified operation.

The balance of the order for ten new cars was soon to hand and these were placed in service as they arrived. Most of the old cars were withdrawn, but four were retained for a short period to be used as required at rush hours. Passengers were, however, content to let the old cars pass then wait for a 'Pullman' to arrive. Here a lady passenger boards car 8 on the inner circle (anticlockwise) in Camelon Road, Larbert. Other than the tram and its track, little has changed since the views shown earlier.

Following the clockwork direction round the circle and recording the new cars in service, car 8 was photographed again, this time in Larbert Main Street, looking towards the station in the distance, where the bulk of the Station Terrace block can again be made out. The entire left (north) side of the street, with these seemingly robust stone-built terraces, has been obliterated – the only unaltered link with the past being the block on the right at the top of Eastcroft Street which has been refurbished in recent years. Perhaps if more of Larbert's old stone buildings had been so treated, its character might also remain.

The canal crossing at Bainsford seems to have acted as a magnet to photographers. This shot, looking east towards the canal terminus at Grangemouth, records the appearance of the new generation of tramcar.

The new tram photographed in Grahams Road, Falkirk about 1930. This forms an interesting contrast with the scene on page 26, and also with the aspect today. The most noticeable change now is the vastly increased volume of road traffic, with it difficult to imagine how the tram could be slotted in now. However, it is only necessary to journey to European cities such as Lisbon or Prague to witness not dissimilar tramcars coping totally successfully with even narrower streets and even more congested traffic conditions. The tram would now be in the middle of the roundabout giving access to the Central Retail Park, while the church behind has also gone.

A period scene looking east along Newmarket Street in the early thirties. Noticeable is the lack of Princes Street at the far end which was not constructed until 1933. This confirms that this photograph dates to between 1930 and 1932. The decorative cast iron railings enclosing the terrace between upper and lower Newmarket Street were removed – supposedly to help the war effort, about 1941, but like most of those removed then, probably remained in enormous piles, rusting and unused as the metal was unsuitable for the purpose intended.

Although the new fleet of Pullman cars initially used the original 1905 depot, in 1931 it was decided that this space would be better used for the ever-expanding bus maintenance facility. A new depot was built some yards further north along Larbert Road. The building still stands, now used by Cockburn Auto Electrics. Until very recently it contained the original tram rails.

Passenger numbers, which had not unnaturally declined during the years of reconstruction, recovered rapidly – so much so that an order was placed for further four cars. These came in August 1931 and were given Nos. 13 – 16, perhaps an indication that two of the old cars were still there at this time as Nos. 11 and 12. Again the passengers would be the first to notice the major change, the use of upholstered transverse seating. The fourteen Pullman cars were all built by the Brush Electrical Engineering Co. of Loughborough in England, where this record photograph was taken of the interior of car 14 before it was despatched north. Remarkably this car still survives.

Car 14 seems to have been remarkably photogenic during its short working life, and is seen again, this time crossing Camelon Canal Bridge on the anticlockwise circle. The four cars with the transverse seats in the saloon were always the most popular, plus they had two seats on the drivers' platform – in theory only those at the conductor's end were in use. At busy times every square inch was occupied, and these cars were renowned for their carrying capacity as well as for their remarkable turn of speed. The close fit between the opening span of the bridge and the roadway will be noted – the cars crossed with an almost imperceptible 'bump'.

The control room of the canal bridge operator in June 1933. By this time the number of openings of the bridge was very much reduced, and the Tramway Company attempted to bring in legislation by promoting a provisional order to restrict the hours of operation. Needless to say the canal's owners, by now the LMS railway company, resisted this absolutely. It was stated in evidence that in 1913, before the First World War, the canal was used by some 11,499 vessels, but that figure had dropped to 3,175 by 1928. The tram undertaking wanted to restrict the hours of operation – based on the reduction in use of the canal – to minimise the cost of manpower necessary to man the operation. Before the First World War, two bridge keepers worked 12 hour shifts for a wage of 15s 0d per week; after (because of the introduction of the 8-hour day) to cope with usage reduced by 72%, three bridge keepers were paid 42s 0d per week. The tramway request was dismissed.

At their first repaint the trams lost the gold lining out, and appeared much less splendiferous in consequence. This interesting view is of a car at the new depot, with two bogies sitting on the adjacent track. Not only has the lining out gone, but the 'legal lettering' is now in miniscule writing on the bottom right-hand corner of the rocker panel. The owners name is now the 'Traction' Company, and the manager is recorded as J Marshall. Douglas Hays was promoted to general manager of the Midland Counties Electric Supply Co. Ltd. which, in addition to a major role in power generation in the Midlands, also

operated the Ilkeston, Notts & Derby and Mansfield tramways (all of which closed in the early 1930s). His successor came from the Dunfermline tramways, where he had been the assistant manager.

Business on the Falkirk circle seemed still to be booming, so in early 1934 five reconditioned second-hand tramcars were added to the fleet. These had had a short previous existence with the Dearne District Light Railways, which had only opened its first route in July 1924, closing at the end of September 1933. Its thirty cars, less than ten years old, were offered for sale. Falkirk obtained five, but it is probable that they did not appreciate the amount of alteration which would be required to allow them to operate on its line. The Dearne cars were long, on four wheeled trucks, but measured 32 feet overall, compared to the 30 feet 6 inches of the bogie cars. In addition to regauging the trucks from 4 feet 8 ½ inches to 4 feet 0 inches, they also had to be shortened from 8 feet 6 inches to 7 feet 4 inches wheel base; the body also needed to be shortened to 28 feet 9 inches to allow the cars to get round the tight radius Falkirk curves. Perhaps they were not the bargain they initially appeared. This is newly delivered car 12, looking quite smart, at the depot in the summer of 1934.

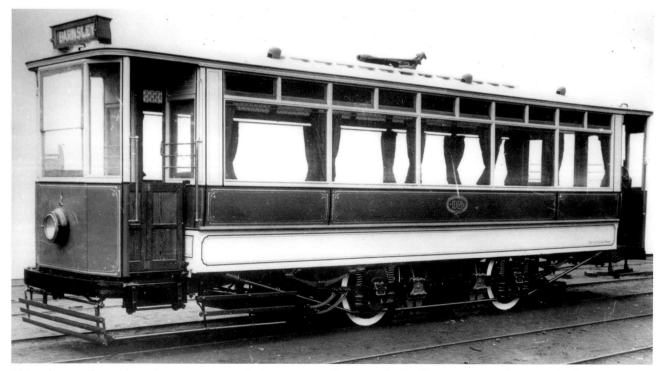

This shows the original appearance of the trams when newly built. By comparison with the preceding photograph, the considerable amount of reconstruction required to adapt the vehicles can be gauged.

Above: The various alterations to shorten the Dearne cars can be clearly seen, but the cost involved cannot have been justified, with the cars giving service for just over two years. Car 11 had a distinctly 'home made' appearance, quite distinct from that of the other four rebuilds.

Opposite above: No. 17 of the Dearne purchase crossing Camelon Canal Bridge. It is working on a 'jerker', from Camelon to Carron via Falkirk and back. At peak periods a five minute frequency service was operated, increased to every four minutes at the week ends. Rosebank Distillery produced a distinctive lowland malt using water from the Carron Valley Reservoir. Originally founded in Laurieston in the early nineteenth century, it was moved to Camelon to ensure a better water supply. Mothballed by then owners Diageo (former Distillers Company) in 1993, most equipment has been removed, much of the site redeveloped and it is unlikely that the site will ever again be used for its original purpose.

Opposite below: To accommodate the five additional cars, a siding was laid outside the depot. Most unusually for a tramway, this incorporated a turntable – seen here at the end of the spur – to allow the cars to be turned end-for-end to allow for equalisation of wear on wheels and bearings. Falkirk's tramway being just the one circular route, this was necessary as otherwise wheels etc on one side would wear out more quickly than the other.

A major improvement to local transport facilities came in 1935 with the opening of the large bus station at Callendar Riggs. By this time most Scottish national bus operations were in the hands of the railway companies, who had exercised powers granted by the 1928 Railway (Road Transport) Acts to work through their nominee companies – the SMT Company in Scotland – to acquire existing operators (in the local area that was W Alexander & Sons Ltd). The operator with the largest fleet and the largest route mileage, the direct descendant of the Tramway Company (the Scottish General Omnibus Company) was absorbed by the monopoly undertaking on 12th June 1930. This unjust arrangement made no concession to primogeniture, or, in fact, to logic. The Alexander name was chosen for reasons which are now lost in the mists of time, but if truth be told the bus empire could have been trading under the 'Scottish General' fleet name, one which would have made a considerably more realistic and have had a greater historic significance. Dunn & Wilson's library and bookshop at the new bus station was a much used facility, and will be fondly remembered by many of Falkirk's Bairns.

The bus of the day is represented (at the new Falkirk bus station) by the Leyland TD2 double decker, which for all its size had only seats for 24 inside and a further 24 on the top deck. This particular vehicle carries an advertisement on the upper deck side panels for 'Aitken's Beer' which was to Falkirk what Guinness is to Dublin, but while the latter flourishes, Aitken's ceased brewing in 1966. The distinctive brewery in Lint Riggs just off Newmarket Street and its landmark red brick chimney were demolished by the army just two years later – the site then sold on to Asda. Local control had been lost from 1960 when the brewery was sold to Caledonian United Breweries. Water for brewing was obtained from 700 feet deep wells on the site, and the undertaking also boasted its own dedicated railway siding, used for direct export of the renowned ale. A well-remembered advertising aphorism was Aitken's use of the illustration of a caged tiger, with the telling slogan 'strength behind bars'.

The successful reconstruction saw passenger numbers rise throughout the early 1930s, reaching nearly four million at the peak. This traffic was viewed with discomfort by the bus operating monopoly which, by June 1935, had purchased 99% of the shares. The successful, well-patronised, modernised tramway was seen as an impediment to 'rationalisation' of bus services; consequently arrangements were immediately put in hand to abandon the service. Car 3 and another with their respective crews are seen as operations drew to a close. Both conductresses have TIMs (Ticket Issuing Machines) which had a short life on the trams, only introduced in March 1933 and discontinued after July 1936.

After reaching agreement with the various local authorities involved it was decided that the last tram would operate on Tuesday 21st July 1936. While this journey started on that date, the car did not reach the confines of the depot until after midnight, hence making the 22nd the precise last day of operation. The last day was wet and miserable, but one or two photographs were made, including this of car 16 on the inner circle entering the west end of Newmarket Street. The notice in the window advises that the trams will operate no more after that day.

The final car was driven by Inspector Walton who had served his entire career with the tramway, and indeed had driven a car on the opening day 31 years previously. A floral wreath was hung from the headlight with the words *At rest: In loving memory. We have had a rattling good time, but owing to modern transport use we have to die, yet were game to the last.* Within three weeks the overhead wires were removed and work followed immediately to remove the rails, starting in Bainsford Main Street. Falkirk Council was paid £5,500 to absolve the bus group from the cost of track removal in the burgh. With the track cast into its concrete foundation, in most places only the upper part of the rail was cut off, the lower half and the concrete foundation remaining to this day over much of the route.

The nineteen redundant trams found no further use – no tramway wanted them second-hand, despite some being only five years old, and they were sold off as garden sheds etc. Not even the electrical equipment was re-

used; the unusual Falkirk 4 feet gauge may have influenced decisions, although the cars would have been equally able to be adapted to run on standard gauge tracks elsewhere. This former Pullman car is but a shadow of its former self, the crisp red paint over-painted green to 'harmonise' with its surroundings at the Carron Valley Reservoir. None of the transport relics which once added to the interest of this spot at the east end of the Campsie Fells now remain. In the thirties and forties the country hut was often a place of weekend escape for a working man; many of these were rough and ready shacks with few amenities. Most have been cleared away in the name of progress.

For many years the circle exhibited a 'ghost' tramway atmosphere as these views show. Here looking south up Vicar Street the short length of the former single line is clear with the latter day double track curve into Newmarket Street equally visible.

The improved bend from Main Street, Camelon north into Larbert Road also shows the evidence of the track layout in this 1939 view. Camelon still retains an important position in public transport as the locus for the bus body building department of Alexanders'. Brown Street was the origin of that organisation, and remained as the headquarters of the organisation through its period of development and change. Note the Belisha crossing on the left, forerunner of today's zebra and other controlled pedestrian crossings. The brainchild in 1934 of Leslie Hore-Belisha the then Minister of Transport (who added the striped pole and flashing orange globe) this gave pedestrians priority over road traffic at these specific points only.

One of the more unusual elements of the fleet of 'vehicles' operated by local transport company was this 62 foot motor vessel *Queen of Loch Earn* which came in with the business of Crerar of Crieff. It was used in connection with tours, and sailed the length of the loch twice daily between 1922 and 1936. Therafter it was tied up at St Fillans and saw out its days as a houseboat.

Falkirk's modern bus station when newly opened – Alexanders' have a complete monopoly.

During the early 1970s the existence of Pullman car 14 was discovered, behind a cottage in the village of Slamannan, some 6½ miles south of Falkirk. The old car was in reasonable condition and the owners, Bobby and Heather Forbes negotiated its future with Jack Sanderson, curator of Falkirk Museum. The outcome of this was the removal in 1978 of the car from a resting place of the best part of 40 years to begin a major restoration project, the removal being recorded for posterity by BBC television cameras.

Interior of the part-restored tram 14 which it is hoped will one day be able to be seen again in the Falkirk district.

THE LAST BUS   FROM GRANGEMOUTH.

WE ALL GO THE SAME WAY HOME.

THE LAST TRAM
From CAMELON.